Effective Pastoral Care Ministry in the Local Church

Kathy J. Smith

Effective Pastoral Care Ministry in the Local Church

Kathy J. Smith

Copyright © 2016 by Kathy J. Smith

ISBN 978-1-61529-175-5

Vision Publishing
1115 D Street
Ramona, CA 92065
1 760 789-4700
www.booksbyvision.com

The Student Study Guide is available from Vision Publishing.

All scripture is from the New American Standard Version unless otherwise noted.

Endorsements

Kathy did an outstanding job of creating a very practical and insightful resource to facilitate the pastoral care in our congregations. We had wanted to find a good pastoral training guide to help resource both our lay pastors and younger pastors, this is the perfect tool for that purpose. As senior pastors we know we can only care for our growing flock as God raises up more people with a nurturing shepherd's heart to sustain and multiply new disciples. This is an excellent book on Pastoral Care in the Local Church; I would highly recommend it for all church staffs and pastors.

Senior Pastors Daniel & Theresa Jones
Summit Church – San Marcos, CA.

"Kathy Smith's book on *Effective Pastoral Care Ministry* is an excellent resource for local churches to assist senior pastors and leaders to meet not only spiritual growth needs for their people, but also mental and emotional care as well. Having a Pastoral Care Ministry in place helps the church grow and become a healthy and strong church in Christ. This book offers a strong basis for the need of pastoral care in the local church."

Drs. Tal and Dee Klaus
Vision International University

In this book, Kathy Smith explains the process of an Effective Pastoral Care Ministry and walks you through it. It's a great read for church follow-up needs. She is a woman with a remarkable ability to write and articulate on how to develop an "Effective Pastoral Care Ministry".

Her life experiences regarding this subject caused the book to come alive and relatable to the reader. It's practical steps are helpful for churches of any denomination. The result of this training is that it causes church growth by touching the congregation and the community through effective pastoral care.

Pastor Anthony & Faye Thomas
Regency Christian Center International
Care Ministry
Whittier, CA

The Study Guide for *Effective Pastoral Care Ministry in the Local Church* is recommended for group study and is available from Vision Publishing at:

1115 D Street
Ramona, CA 92065
760 789-4700

Contact <u>Rebecca@vision.edu</u> or <u>ksmith@vision.edu</u>
to order your copy.

Table of Contents

Foreword

One of the most important roles for a pastor is the care of God's people. Pastors are referred to as shepherds in scripture, with a primary responsibility of providing guidance (leading), nurture (feeding and teaching), and protection from the wolves of the world. Pastoral care is critical to the growth and sustaining of Christ's church; unfortunately, due to many reasons this area of responsibility is neglected.

One primary reason is the unreasonable expectation God's people have of a local Pastor. Pastors are looked to for more than teaching the principles of God's word and guiding God's people with wisdom. They are looked at as the first source of advice for marriage, financial concerns, petty business squabbles, etc. Thus no individual pastor with a congregation of over seventy can give healthy Pastoral Care; what pastors need is a team to help in the nurture and care of the church.

Rev. Kathy Smith is a true expert in the training and development of Pastoral Care Teams. She doesn't just talk about it; she has developed and led teams for many years. She articulates the wisdom of experience and biblical knowledge into her book and teaching, *Effective Pastoral Care in the Local Church.*

Her passion is to see churches fully resourced and pastors completely supported by raising up power teams to empower God's people. If you have a hunger for personal ministry for the flock of God, if your desire is to be equipped for effective pastoral care service, this is the book and course for you.

Sincerely in Christ,

Stan E. DeKoven Ph.D. Author of *Leadership in the Church*

A Word from the Author

Write the vision. Make it plain. Pastoral care ministry benefits the church and its constituency, as well as the team members delivering the care. Personal spiritual growth, corporate body growth and healing for the hurting are just a few of the many benefits that can be gleaned from participation on a pastoral care team.

The objective of this book is to paint a picture of effective pastoral care; using your mind as the canvas and revelation as the brush, to impart the vision. Proverbs 29:18 (KJV) states: "Without a vision the people perish." The NASB states, "Where there is no vision (revelation) the people go unrestrained." Without vision, people have no direction, like a river with no shore, left to wander aimlessly without guidance or parameters.

How can one prepare, strategize, and enact a plan that will take you to the finish line if you have no vision to guide you? Habakkuk said, write the vision. Why? So that he who reads it may run with it. We want you to run with it, so the impartation is imminent. We wish to impress upon your own personal canvas, a vision for effective pastoral care. It is then your responsibility to act on the vision, pick up the baton and run the race. Now is the time to make it happen; as we endeavor to do the work of the Lord.

See you at the finish line! God Speed!

Rev. Kathy J Smith —Doctoral Candidate

Vision International University

www.planpurposedestiny.org

Introduction

Which word best describes your church?
Is it a lighthouse, hospital, or sanctuary?

Churches by definition are expected to be a safe haven for the lost, hurting, and injured. The body of Christ is to be a place of healing in times of trouble. In his book, *The Healing Community,* Dr. Stan DeKoven wrote, "One of the historical functions of church life and the role of pastoral ministry is to provide healing for the wounded soul. Although most churches and pastors agree with the need to assist the discouraged and dysfunctional in the congregation, few churches and pastors are adequately equipped for the task."[1]

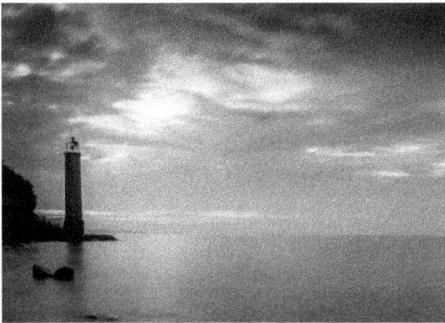

The word sanctuary, the word we often use to refer to the room where we hold our weekly worship services, also means: "a place of refuge or safety. Synonyms are haven, harbor, port in a storm, oasis, shelter, retreat, hideaway, hideout..."[2]

Many churches are trying to do more for their constituents and their community during times of significant life challenges to promote healing and restore health. In recent history, many churches have expected the senior pastors to shoulder much of the

---

[1] *The Healing Community* by Dr. Stan DeKoven and published by Vision Publishing is available at http://www.booksbyvision.com/index.php?route=product/product&product_id=295

[2] Google definitions https://www.google.com/webhp?sourceid=chrome-instant&ion=1&espv=2&ie=UTF-8#safe=active&q=sanctuary+definition

burden for such care on their own. This is neither reasonable nor healthy. It creates a situation where too often, people wind up slipping through the cracks.

Which word best describes your church? I trust that it is all three: a lighthouse to the lost, a hospital for the sick and injured, and a sanctuary for those seeking safety. If it is not, it needs to be. It is for this reason we come together to discuss the responsibilities of the church, the church leadership, and the laity in providing the needed care. The sanctuary is more than just a place to hold a weekly worship service; it is a safe haven where health is restored and healing is renewed.

Rev. Kathy J. Smith

Rev. Kathy J. Smith

Why is Pastoral Care Important?

To Avoid Losing People in the Cracks

This is what the people in the community could be saying about your church...........

- "I wish my church was as supportive and caring as your church!"

- "That church knows how to love on its congregation! What a fantastic group of people."

- "Your church is the best cared for flock in the region!"

A good quality Pastoral Care Ministry can decrease the incidence of people going MIA inside the four walls of your local church. What is a MIA you might ask? MIAs are the people of your body that are **Missing in Action.** You know, those people that come to visit once, twice, or maybe even three times; and then they are never seen again. Or perhaps they have been attending for some time and have become involved in some ministry projects within the body. Then one day they are simply not there anymore. The pew where they sat is empty, their place in the ministry unfilled.

We have all seen them. Where do these people go? Did anyone take the time to inquire? Did they move? Get a new job? Have a family crisis that keeps them away? Was something said or done that hurt or offended them? Without good follow-up care many of these people simply fall through the cracks. We are losing too many people to the cracks! Isn't it time we show these people we really do care?

People can say that they care all they want, but when the community sees that your church lives what they believe, they will stand up and take notice. What better testimony can one give? The widows are cared for, the sick are visited, the people in the hospitals are tended to and their families are given the loving support they deserve.

The staff at the hospital will begin to notice. The staff in the nursing homes will begin to notice. The family members of those being cared for will begin to notice. Even the funeral home directors will begin to talk when they see what wonderful care your people are being given. Pretty soon everyone in the community will have heard about your church. With a reputation like this, what is to stop your church from growing?

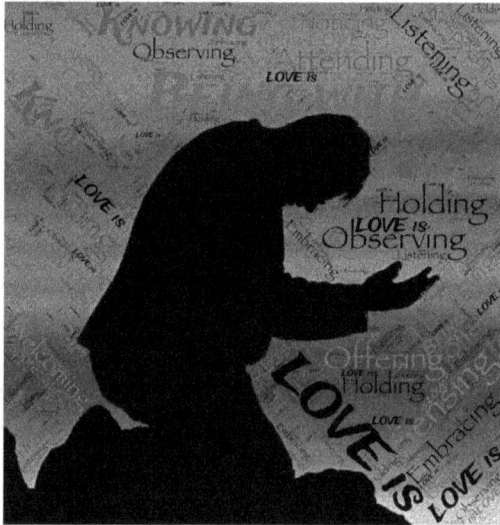

What Does the Lord Require?

There was a day when many felt that attending church once a week and paying their tithe, was all that was required. If they fulfilled this, then they had satisfied their obligations to God. Even today, many are of that opinion. That is not exactly what God had in mind. He wants more than a superficial, long distance relationship with his kids.

He wants to get up close and personal. He wants a one on one intimate relationship. Mere church attendance or payment of the weekly tithe fails to produce the type of relationship our loving Father seeks to have with each of us.

Just think of it, what kind of a relationship would a married couple have if they merely met once a week to discuss family affairs and place money in the bank to pay the bills? After the weekly commitment they each go their separate way to do as they wish. That would be a really crummy marriage! God wants more for us and from us as well.

The fact that you are reading this book to learn about Pastoral Care Ministry indicates to me that your commitment to the Lord and to doing his work have moved past mere church attendance. You have ventured beyond just hearing of the word, and you have moved into the arena of "doing" it.

I beseech you therefore, brethren, by the mercies of God, that ye present your bodies a living sacrifice, holy, acceptable unto God, which is your reasonable service.

Romans 12:1

For some, being <u>fully</u> committed to the Lord may seem like a tall order. After all, there are other commitments such as work, school, and family to take into consideration. What does it mean to be fully committed to the Lord? Does it mean we need to withdraw from society and spend our days in prayer and fasting? Or do we need to give up our worldly possessions and travel to the mission field to devote our lives to God and others?

No, of course not, not unless you were specifically called to devote your life to such endeavors; but for most of us, it merely means that he expects us to love him with all of our heart, with all of our mind, and with all of our soul.[3] He desires to be number one in our life. We are to seek him, his kingdom and his righteousness; and when we do; he will be our all in all. He becomes our ultimate source.

Love Your Neighbor as Yourself

Then the righteous will answer Him, 'Lord, when did we see You hungry, and feed You, or thirsty, and give You something to drink? And when did we see You a stranger, and invite You in, or naked, and clothe You? When did we see You sick, or in prison, and come to You?' The King will answer and say to them, 'Truly I say to you, to the extent that you did it to one of these brothers of Mine, even the least of them, you did it to Me.'

Matthew 25:37-40

"Teacher, which is the great commandment in the Law?" And He said to him,

"'YOU SHALL LOVE THE LORD YOUR GOD WITH ALL YOUR HEART, AND WITH ALL YOUR SOUL, AND WITH ALL YOUR MIND.'

"This is the great and foremost commandment."The second is like it, 'YOU SHALL LOVE YOUR NEIGHBOR AS YOURSELF.' "On these two commandments depend the whole Law and the Prophets."

---

[3] See Matthew 22:37

Matthew 22:36-40

Pure and undefiled religion in the sight of our God and Father is this: to visit orphans and widows in their distress, and to keep oneself unstained by the world.

James 1:27

What does he require of us? He requires that we love one another just as he first loved us. We are to love one another, even as we love ourselves. He is the head but he needs us to be his hands, his feet, and his body. Time is of the essence; we must <u>be</u> the church not merely attend church.

What did Jesus tell Peter to do just before he ascended? He said three times, "Peter, **feed my sheep.**" How can we feed and care for his sheep? We can care for them by becoming active in Pastoral Care Ministry.

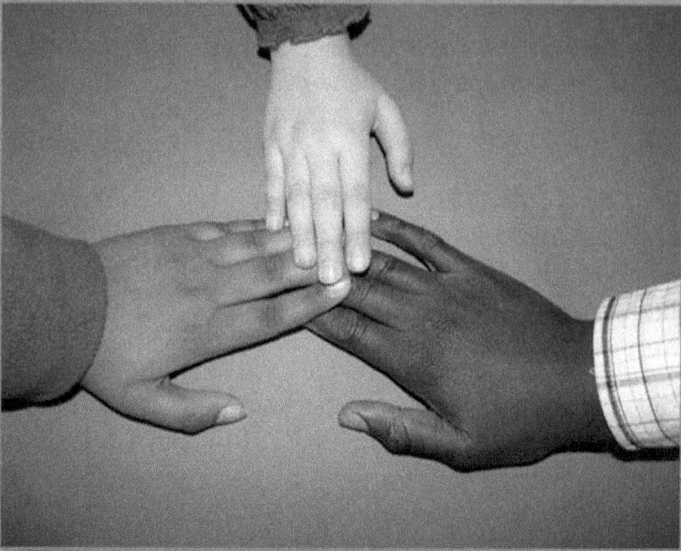

What Does the Lord Require?

Feed My Sheep

What is Pastoral Care Ministry?

"... But God has so composed the body, giving more abundant honor to that member which lacked, so that there may be no division in the body, but that the members may have the same care for one another. And if one member suffers, all the members suffer with it; if one member is honored, all the members rejoice with it."

1 Corinthians 12:24-27

Let us begin by defining the term pastoral care. Pastoral care is the mental, emotional and spiritual support given to others in times of need. This is accomplished through the vehicle of the church lay ministry. Offering a listening ear, a soft shoulder to cry on, words of encouragement and hope; and most importantly, prayer. These are just a few of the ways that lay leaders on the pastoral care team may find themselves lending a helping hand.

Let's face it, life just happens and crisis comes. Not one of us is immune. No one plans to have a crisis. Disaster always knocks on the front door uninvited; and when it does, we really need one another. Deuteronomy 32:30 states one can put a thousand to flight, two 10,000. Ecclesiastes 4:12 states a three-fold cord is not easily broken.

The storms of life produce heartaches appearing as clouds of despair. The clouds of despair are seeded with lies from the enemy that produce doubt. Left unchallenged, doubt will threaten the destruction of our hope and dreams; therefore, we must stand firm on the word of the Lord. It is in those trying times that we are better together. We need one another.

When we are connected to each other through relationship, no one needs to fear the storm. When one is weak, the others are strong. We can stand firm in our mutual faith. We truly are better together. Pastoral Care ministry team members keep others who have been weakened by life events from falling. No one needs to fall through the cracks.

What is a pastoral care ministry team? It is a group of trained lay leaders who care. Do you care about your brothers and sisters in the Lord? Do you care about people outside of the church who come to you hurting? Indifference robs us of compassion. We cannot minister effectively if we do not care. Compassion is the expression of God's love to those who are hurting and in need. Compassion, mercy, and grace are required to effectively fulfill a role in the PCM.

At times, good godly people through no fault of their own, find themselves in trying circumstances. It may be a bad medical report, a car accident, or a death in the family; these are just a few among the many possibilities. At other times, people make bad choices; they invite trouble into their home. Then when circumstances manifest into a crisis, they need help. Where do they turn? They turn to the church.

While we do not condone sin, or encourage sinful living, we are required to love the sinner. Jesus did. So must we. We must show them the love of God no matter what they have done or where they have been. This requires a heart of compassion; it is the love of Christ flowing through each of us. We need to care for our fellow man. Another term we could use for pastoral care is care giving. We are care givers to those who need hope, help, healing and encouragement.

While in some churches pastoral care is considered the sole responsibility of the senior pastors, no church pastor can sustain a growing number of members and hope to offer sufficient care for all the needs of the people. Those that try will quickly find that their own personal prayer and bible study time will begin to suffer. Tending to the tables takes time (Acts 6).For others, responsibilities to spouse, family and significant others will be neglected to provide the needed care to hurting church members. This is unbalanced and unhealthy for all.

A healthy church is one in which the senior pastors have equipped and empowered mature seasoned lay leaders to help tend to the needs of the flock. Once such a team is in place, the senior pastors have the needed support to sustain the ministry even in times of exponential growth.

Review

The Pastoral Care Ministry is a <u>network</u> of lay people, hand chosen for the express purpose of ministering to the body. As the church begins to grow in size, the responsibilities of caring for the flock can become increasingly more challenging.

Maintaining good quality follow-up for the <u>sick</u>, the <u>widows</u>, and the <u>elderly</u> can become increasingly more difficult and even burdensome at times when it is the sole responsibility of the Pastors. That is why it becomes imperative that the Pastors develop a network of lay ministers to support them in the work of the ministry.[4]

Discussion

- Why have you chosen to be a part of the pastoral care ministry team?

- What would you like to learn about pastoral care ministry?

- How do you believe a good pastoral care ministry can benefit you, your church and the community?

---

[4] Those who are using the student study guide, the fill-ins for this section of the guide are underlined above.

The History of Pastoral Care

Pastoral Care Ministry is not a new concept. Biblical roots shaped and defined pastoral care in the modern day church. We find in Exodus, God had entrusted the responsibility of caring for the whole nation of Israel to his friend Moses. He quickly became overwhelmed from sitting and hearing the matters of the people from morning till night.

> *Now when Moses' father-in-law saw all that he was doing for the people, he said, "What is this thing that you are doing for the people? Why do you alone sit as judge and all the people stand about you from morning until evening?*

Exodus 18:14

Jethro counseled Moses in the following verses:

> *"and Moses' father-in-law said to him, "The thing that you are doing is not good. You will surely wear out, both yourself and these people who are with you, for the task is too heavy for you; you cannot do it alone. Now listen to me: I will give you counsel, and God be with you. You be the people's representative before God, and you bring the disputes to God, then teach them the statutes and the laws, and make known to them the way in which they are to walk and the work they are to do.*

> *Furthermore, you shall select out of all the people able men who fear God, men of truth, those who hate dishonest gain; and you shall place these over them as leaders of thousands, of hundreds of fifties and of tens. Let them judge the people at all times; and let it be that every major dispute they will bring to you, but every minor dispute they themselves will judge. So it will be easier for you, and they will bear the burden with you. If you do this thing and God so commands*

you, then you will be able to endure, and all these people also will go to their place in peace."

Exodus 18:17-23

Jethro's advice was four fold.

1. You be a <u>representative</u> of the people to God.

   Moses was to be an advocate. He heard the people's concerns and conveyed those concerns to the Lord. He would reason with the Lord at times for mercy for the people.

2. <u>Teach</u> the people God's statutes and laws.

   Moses was responsible for teaching the people those things they needed to know to adhere to the laws and statutes instituted by God.

3. <u>Delegate</u>. Select honest, God fearing leaders to take responsibility for the people. He was to create an organizational chart of leaders who would take responsibility for those entrusted to their care.

4. <u>Empower</u>. Give them the responsibility of thousands, of hundreds of fifties and of tens.

In Acts 6 of the New Testament we find another example of leadership being overwhelmed by the needs of the people.

The problem:

Now at this time while the disciples were increasing in number, a complaint arose on the part of the Hellenistic Jews against the native Hebrews, because their widows were being overlooked in the daily serving of food. So the twelve summoned the congregation of the disciples and said, "It is not desirable for us to neglect the word of God in order to serve tables.

The solution:

Therefore, brethren, select from among you seven men of good reputation, full of the Spirit and of wisdom, whom we may put in charge of this task. But we will devote ourselves to prayer and to the ministry of the word."

The lay ministry chosen, empowered, and released for service:

The statement found approval with the whole congregation; and they chose Stephen, a man full of faith and of the Holy Spirit, and Philip, Prochorus, Nicanor, Timon, Parmenas and Nicolas, a proselyte from Antioch. And these they brought before the apostles; and after praying, they laid their hands on them.

Once again we see in the New Testament a pattern for delegation of authority as it pertains to church government. Those who are ultimately responsible to the Lord for the people entrusted to them, must equip, empower, and release others to do the work of the ministry.

In his book, Leadership in the Church Dr. Stan DeKoven wrote,

"Luke 2:52 best illustrates the need of preparation for ministry.

"And Jesus increased in wisdom and stature, and in favor with God and man," (KJV).

If Jesus needed to grow in His preparation before His release into ministry, how much more do potential leaders need to grow as members of His Kingdom? He grew in all aspects of His life, mentally, emotionally, socially, and spiritually. Thus, the leader's preparation is vital."[5]

Before and during seasons of church growth it is the primary responsibility of those in five-fold ministry positions to educate lay

---

[5] *Leadership In The Church* by Dr. Stan DeKoven published by Vision Publishing of Ramona, CA 92065 www.booksbyvision.com

leaders to help with the growing responsibilities of caring for those in the church as seen in the early church. Only then can the church continue to grow in maturity and stature.

Discussion

- How are the problems of Moses in his leadership role with the nation of Israel and the problems of the disciples in the early church, similar to problems faced day in and day out by the senior pastors of the present day church?

- There is a chain of command defined in the biblical examples we just read. How is their chain of command similar or different from the model being used in your own church?

- Why is it important to follow the chain of command by reporting your concerns to the appropriate leader? Who has the ultimate responsibility for the care of the congregation?

Released to Serve

And these they brought before the apostles; and after praying, they laid their hands on them.

Act 6:6

Chain of Command

Understanding the hierarchy of responsibility and the chain of command in any organization is the key to its success. Moses had to delegate his authority to others. He did so by creating a chain of command. He empowered the leaders that would ultimately report to him, and he reported to God. Each of those leaders had to do the same for those under them. They choose their own leaders and assigned them their own portion of responsibility. Each leader delegated authority to others under them until the people were grouped in manageable units to adequately care for all of their needs.

Churches and the ministries within the church must have an organizational structure if it is to operate smoothly. God is a God of order. Following the proper chain of authority is extremely important.

The following diagrams (pg. 31, 32) will help you visualize the flow of authority from the head down. You will also see the significance of a pastoral care ministry in the growth of the church. We will use a tree in the first diagram to represent the church. Although the analogy is not 100 % accurate, it is close enough to help us understand more fully how PCM promotes church growth.

On the left side of the diagram that follows, the barren tree signifies a brand new church plant. The new tree has not yet had the opportunity to produce foliage or fruit. The root bulb we will identify as the pastors and other church leadership. This new church plant shows no evidence of new root growth, fruit, or foliage.

The tree to the right in this same diagram is a church that has already begun to grow. The leadership (the tree bulb) has developed significantly creating a root system which we will refer to as the PCM. A healthy root system (PCM) will help support and nurture the growth of the visible church, the people, and will eventually produce fruit. Of course ultimately the church is rooted and grounded in Christ.

It is important to understand that the growth first begins from being rooted in the Lord. Then the pastors and other five-fold ministry form the church leadership (the tree bulb). They have their authority directly from the Lord as they remain rooted and grounded in him.

The new root growth is an extension of the leadership, although not one in the same. The only authority given to the PCM is that which is given to it by the church leadership. The pastoral team cannot stand alone. The role of the PCM is highly significant but the work is often behind the scenes. Accolades may come privately from those they help, or through the affirmation of the leadership. Those who desire public affirmations may not be well suited to this ministry.

Discussion

- Describe the chain of command in your own church body.

- Who are you directly responsible to for the work you do in PCM?

- Why is important to report directly to the Pastoral Director rather than others?

Church Plant

Growing Church

New Church Plant

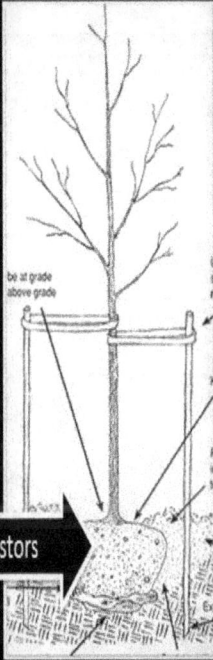

be at grade
above grade

Pastors

Church Congregation
(growth and fruit bearing)

Senior pastors (tree bulb)

PCM lay leaders (root system)

Rooted and grounded in the Lord

The diagram below also shows the chain of command in church government. This time it is represented in a pyramid style sketch. Once again the Lord is the ultimate authority and he empowers the pastors and other five-fold ministry to do the work upon the earth. It is their job to equip, delegate, and release those they choose to assist in the everyday needs of the church body.

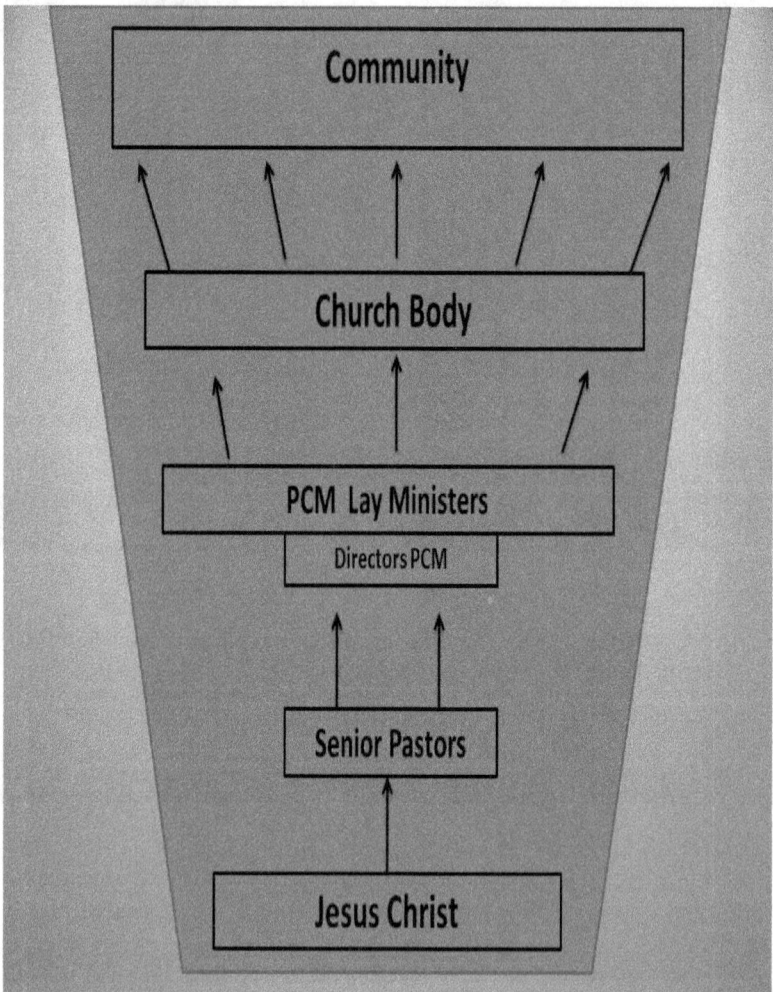

Spiritual Anatomy

A number of years ago, before I began working at Vision International, I supported myself by working as a registered nurse. One of my favorite subjects in nursing school was anatomy and physiology. I was fascinated by the intricacy with which the body had been created. Each organ system had its own specific components and they worked together to fulfill the function for which they were created.

No body system is capable of standing on its own; each individual system needs to partner with others. The circulatory system needs the respiratory system, and the nervous system needs the skeletal system, and so on. Each one is necessary if the body is to function effectively.

A good nursing assessment is based upon the standards established for a healthy body. An abnormality in the patient's condition is anything outside of the established norm. Therefore, knowledge of anatomy and physiology is necessary for a proper assessment of the patient's needs and consequently the giving of appropriate care.

Connecting Member To Member and Bone To Bone

The human body is made up of many different members, as is the body of Christ. As members of Christ's body, it is important that we understand how and where we fit together. We need to understand what each person's role is, his or her responsibilities, and how that role and function fit seamlessly with others to form the body of Christ.

> *For even as the body is one and yet has many members, and all the members of the body, though they are many, are one body, so also is Christ.*

1 Corinthians 12:12

How do my calling, my purpose, and my gifts benefit my brothers and sisters in the Lord? How do they benefit the body as a whole? My relationship to others can and does affect the whole body.

Where Do I Fit?

Many Christians are currently suffering an identity crisis. They do not understand who they are or what role they play, much less how to help others find their place. The people perish for lack of knowledge.[6] Knowledge of one's personal identity begins with a personal relationship with the Lord. As one's relationship with the Lord matures, a greater understanding of personal calling and identity become apparent.

Lay leaders and especially members of the five-fold ministry are responsible for helping others find their proper place within the body. Knowing how and where people fit together requires a clear understanding of the anatomy and physiology of the body; I like to call it spiritual anatomy.

First, let us review the scriptures found in Ezekiel 37 regarding dry bones. In this text, God has a conversation with Ezekiel about the bones in the valley. He tells Ezekiel to prophesy to the bones. It is important to note that this thought did not originate with Ezekiel, but with God. God told him what to say. Ezekiel did not conjure this concept up on his own. He merely spoke what he heard the Father speak. We cannot simply name and claim whatever blessing we desire, but rather we must speak the words and the will of the Father. John in chapter 12:49-50 relates the words of Jesus:

> *For I did not speak on My own initiative, but the Father Himself who sent Me has given Me a commandment as to what to say and what to speak. I know that His commandment is eternal life; therefore the things I speak, I speak just as the Father has told Me."*

---

[6]   Hosea 4:6 (Knowledge can be acquired via a relationship with the Lord.)

Again in John 5:19:

Therefore Jesus answered and was saying to them, "Truly, truly, I say to you, the Son can do nothing of Himself, unless it is something He sees the Father doing; for whatever the Father does, these things the Son also does in like manner.

Ezekiel prophesied to the dead bones and they came together. The illustration of dead bones coming together is a reference to the promise of God in the preceding chapter. He promised the restoration of the nation of Israel. They would be gathered together again from the places where they had been scattered.

Secondly, we can see this representation being carried even further to symbolize the restoration of the body of Christ. The members of his body were once dead in their sin but are promised resurrection and newness of life in Christ Jesus.[7] Consequently, we can deduce that the bones are representatives of the members of the body, as are you and I. We are the bones of the body of Christ.

Bones Come Together at Joints

Bones of the body come together at junctions better known as joints. The joints where the bones meet are relationships; relationships we have with one another. It is at the joint of relationship where we come together to form the body of Christ. It is our relationships that hold us together or can potentially pull us apart. The joints[8] supply the needs of the body as a whole.

From whom the whole body, fitly joined together and compacted by that which every joint supplieth, according to the effectual working in the measure of every part, maketh increase of the body unto the edifying of itself in love.

Ephesians 4:16

---

[7] See the commentary of Matthew Henry on Ezekiel 37.

[8] Mature/ healthy relationships

This is a powerful verse. It contains enough spiritual food for a whole month of Sundays! You may want to refer to an interlinear bible to look up the original meaning of the words. For instance, the word "whole" in the original Greek means: to join closely together, to frame together parts of a building, or the members of a body. Therefore, we can say that the "whole body" is those members of the body that have been framed or fit together. The verse repeats this in the next phrase, "fitly joined together."

When a builder constructs the framework for a building, he creates the structure by joining boards together at joints; so must the body of Christ be fit together. If the framework of a building is to fit together properly, the boards must be measured and adjusted individually so that they fit snuggly enough to support one another. If the angle is not just right, the union between two boards will not be strong enough to support the structure. If someone mixes up the boards and connects the wrong ones together, it can be a disaster. Each one must fit into the specific location for which it was created.

This same analogy can be seen in the physical body. Try fitting a hipbone into a shoulder socket, or the index finger into the hip, it does not work. They need to be fit together in the proper order. Bones that are out of place are referred to as disjointed.

When something becomes disjointed, it can cause the whole body a great deal of discomfort and pain. Not to mention the fact that it can no longer function at full capacity. In order for the physical body to function at the maximum level and strength, every bone must be in the appropriate place.

Have you ever seen someone try to function in a gift or role in the church that was clearly not theirs? For instance, the church member that is highly gifted as an usher or sound technician may make a very poor administrator. The tone deaf Sunday school teacher may be an excellent educator but should not direct the church choir.

People who are out of place or missing cause the whole body to suffer. We are told not to forsake the assembling of ourselves, for each member is needed.[9] Each member supplies a gift and nourishment for the body. When one part is missing or out of place, the whole body functions less effectively. We need each other.

Let us examine this scripture further, *"fitly joined together and compacted by that which every joint supplieth."* Bones or members that are fit together properly, create joints that are not only compacted, but also supply the needs of the body. The joint serves as a point of connection where an exchange can take place and needs can be met.

How could your forearm function properly if your lower arm is missing or injured? Pushing, pulling, or picking up an object would be difficult if not impossible. When both are in place and healthy, the joint supplies the needs of the body and gives it full functionality.

If one of the members of the body should become sick or diseased, then it will not only affect that specific part, but it will also affect the body as a whole. When one member hurts, we all hurt.

So how do the joints supply the needs of others? We minister to one another through the use of our gifts and our talents as we come together in relationships. It is our gifts from God that give us the ability to minister to the needs of others in the body of Christ. Therefore, our relationships with one another and with God are very important to the overall wellbeing of the whole church.

What Are Sinews?

We have discussed bones and joints, but the body is made up of more than bones and joints. The scripture in Ezekiel said that God was putting sinews on them. What are sinews? The Strong's

---

[9]   Hebrews 10:25

concordance defines this word as a tendon. Tendons and ligaments support the union of two bones at a joint. What supports our relationships in the body of Christ? We must come together in right attitudes toward one another. The scriptures regarding attitudes are numerous, but we will delve into a few.

> *"This is My commandment, that you love one another, just as I have loved you." Love one another... just as Jesus Christ loves you?*

John 15:12

We all know how difficult that can be at times. Loving someone who may have used and abused you, loving someone in spite of differences; but still, we must love. Even when we do not feel we have the love within us, we can make a choice to love with the love of the Lord.

God loves all of humanity and died for us while we were still sinners. We have the God of love living on the inside of us, so we can choose to love with a God kind of love. That does not mean that we must tolerate abuse. Sometimes we must love from afar. Nevertheless, we have been commanded to love.

The Attitude of Christ

Jesus, using the little children that clamored about him as living examples, taught his disciples a valuable kingdom lesson. What type of attitude are we to have? Those who are greatest in the kingdom shall become like the little children and humble themselves....

> *At that time the disciples came to Jesus and said, "Who then is greatest in the kingdom of heaven?" And He called a child to Himself and set him before them, and said, "Truly I say to you, unless you are converted and become like children, you will not enter the kingdom of heaven. Whoever then humbles himself as this child, he is the greatest in the kingdom of*

heaven. And whoever receives one such child in My name receives Me;

Matthew 18:1-5

Paul also wrote of this kingdom principal in Philippians 2:5 saying this, *"Have this attitude in yourselves which was also in Christ Jesus."* What attitude? Let us back up two verses to gain a better understanding of what he is referring to here.

Do nothing from selfishness or empty conceit, but with humility of mind regard one another as more important than yourselves; do not merely look out for your own personal interests, but also for the interests of others.

Philippians 2:3-4

Paul was instructing us to have an attitude of humility. We are to look at others as being more important than ourselves. Jesus demonstrated humility throughout his life. The very act of laying down his own deity to become a man was the purest form of humility. Then again, the act of laying down his life to die on the cross and taking our punishment, donning a towel to wash the feet of the disciples, and the examples go on. We are to be humble, we are to love, and we are to forgive.

The Forgiveness Factor -- Seventy Times Seven

Then Peter came and said to Him, "Lord, how often shall my brother sin against me and I forgive him? Up to seven times?" Jesus said to him, "I do not say to you, up to seven times, but up to seventy times seven.

Matthew 18:21-22

This is not to say that we are to continue to forgive when the sin against you is repeated and the sinner does not repent of his wrongdoing. This can be seen in Luke 17:3, "Be on your guard! If your brother sins, rebuke him; and if he repents, forgive him." The key here is the sincerity of the repentance. We are not to be a doormat for abuse.

The necessity of forgiveness was frequently taught during Jesus' ministry on the earth. He spoke of it in the Lord's Prayer.

> *Whenever you stand praying, forgive, if you have anything against anyone, so that your Father who is in heaven will also forgive you your transgressions.*

Mark 11:25

Forgiveness is the underlying theme of the whole bible. We have the free gift of forgiveness, not by works but by grace. Therefore, even as we have received forgiveness, we are to forgive.

Ligaments and Tendons Added At Joints for Strength and Support

The whole body is being held together by the ligaments and tendons according to Colossians 2:19:

> *And not holding fast to the head, from whom the entire body, being supplied and held together by the joints and ligaments, grows with a growth which is from God.*

The source of our strength is Jesus Christ; he is the head of the body. From him comes nourishment that supplies all of our needs. As long as we remain in him, and he in us, we have a continuous supply to meet every need. The joints and the ligaments hold the bones of the body together.

Once again, the bones are the individual members of the body of Christ, the members come together at the joints which are relationships. When relationships are strengthened by right attitudes, the whole body is strengthened. Alone we are vulnerable, but together we are whole. We were created for unity. We were created for relationship.

For just as we have many members in one body and all the members do not have the same function so we, who are many, are one body in Christ, and individually members one of another.

Romans 12:4-5

Covering of Flesh and Skin

Once again, Ezekiel tells us how the bones were covered with flesh and skin. In keeping with the analogy of the human body, what might the flesh and skin represent in the body of Christ? For one thing, we know that we are held together by a bond of peace. Let us examine another scripture that focuses on the concept presented in this chapter.

With all humility and gentleness, with patience, showing tolerance for one another in love, being diligent to preserve the unity of the Spirit in the bond of peace.

Ephesians 4:2-3

We see how right attitudes including: humility, patience, and love maintained in a bond of peace can strengthen the whole body. The bond of peace is similar to the covering of flesh. The skin, the ultimate bond, is love. We are to love one another. At the end of the day, it is love through faith holding us all together.

Then The Breath Came In To Them

Ezekiel prophesied to the four winds and breath came into them, and they came alive. The wind is symbolic of God's spirit. Like mouth-to-mouth resuscitation, the breath revived the dead bones and they stood on their feet as a mighty army. In Act 2, the disciples are awaiting the promise of God; then a mighty rushing wind came in to the upper room. They were endued with power from on high. The awaited promise had come.

Conclusion

Some bones are more closely related and have more in common with one another, than others. Some of the bones come together and form a Baptist church; some form a Lutheran church, and some form a Pentecostal or Charismatic church.

Even in one local body, we have many different bones that come together, yet we are not all alike. Not all are noses, ears, or eyes. Not all are the leg, the arm, or the hand. Yet God has placed us together as he wills.

> *"If they were all one member, where would the body be? Now there are many members but one body.*

I Corinthians 12:19-20

How do the bones come together in their proper place? A physical building must be framed by construction workers or builders. Builders that frame the spiritual church are members of the five-fold ministry. They function as the hand of God, working as his spiritual body builders to strengthen, equip, and place the church in order.

> *And He gave some as apostles, and some as prophets, and some as evangelists, and some as pastors and teachers, for the equipping of the saints for the work of service, to the building up of the body of Christ;*

Ephesians 4:11-12

The word "equip" in this verse means to set in place, to fit together, to set in order, to mend, to prepare. Like framing a house or setting a bone. The bones in the body must be fit together in the proper order by God's body building five-fold ministry.

Believers must be trained and equipped. Immature believers are not ready to fulfill their calling; they need mature believers to mentor them, hence the five-fold ministry.

... until we all attain to the unity of the faith, and of the knowledge of the Son of God, to a mature man, to the measure of the stature which belongs to the fullness of Christ.

Ephesians 4:13

From dead bones to lively army: tendons, ligaments, bones, and skin; the body of Christ can be resurrected and walk in the newness of life. Love holds us together.

So, as those who have been chosen of God, holy and beloved, put on a heart of compassion, kindness, humility, gentleness and patience; bearing with one another, and forgiving each other, whoever has a complaint against anyone; just as the Lord forgave you, so also should you. Beyond all these things put on love, which is the perfect bond of unity. Let the peace of Christ rule in your hearts, to which indeed you were called in one body; and be thankful.

Colossian 3:12-15

Discussion

- In your own words, explain the anatomy of the body of Christ.

- How are right attitudes important to the functioning of the church body?

Have you got your love on?

Beyond all these things put on love,
which is the perfect bond of unity.

Colossians 3:14

What is Body Ministry?

We are all one body, but that one body is made up of many different members.[10] Some of us have gifts of administration or teaching, while others are equipped in the areas of helps, giving, or mercy. None of us is totally self-sufficient on our own, but as we come together in Christ we become whole. As we minister to one another within the capability of our own gifts, each joint will supply a need.

Pastoral Care Ministry, PCM, is the epitome of body ministry. Our primary concern is to minister to the body of believers while upholding and supporting the Senior Pastors. Their role is to lead the congregation into greater endeavors for the kingdom of God. Our role is to support them much as Aaron and Hur supported the arms of Moses when they became heavy.[11] We hold up their arms as they lead the congregation.

It is important to keep priorities and responsibilities in order regarding our assistance in caring for the flock. We need to remember that we are merely assisting the senior pastors with their responsibilities. They are ultimately responsible to God for the care of the congregation. As members of the PCM we are first and foremost responsible to the senior pastor, not to the congregation.

Pastoral ministry members have the authority given to them by the leadership. Pastoral ministry PCM is not a pulpit ministry and has no administrative authority. It is the responsibility of the PCM team member to maintain good communication; keeping leader-

---

[10] Romans 12:12-14

[11] Exodus 17:12"But Moses' hands were heavy. Then they took a stone and put it under him, and he sat on it; and Aaron and Hur supported his hands, one on one side and one on the other. Thus his hands were steady until the sun set."

ship updated on all ministry activities. This is done through the timely filing of pastoral reports.

The PCM can be likened to our own nervous system; it keeps our brain informed about what is happening in the various parts of our physical body. When our foot hurts, the brain knows it because our own nervous system communicates that information. When it is pinched or stepped on, the nervous system transmits a pain impulse to the brain. The brain then responds by pulling the foot back and preventing further pain. Effective communication is the key to maintaining a healthy church.

Sensitive Issues

We must endeavor to maintain a sense of peace, unity and harmony. This pertains to relationships with individual members of the body, but also the members as they relate to church leadership. We want to discourage idle gossip. When serious concerns are being conveyed in regards to the intent, actions, or words of the pastor or anyone else in the congregation, exercise caution. If you can quietly diffuse the situation with facts you can share, then do so; but do not allow the conversation to escalate to an argument. You are not there to defend the pastor or other leaders; neither should you entertain ongoing conversation of a negative nature.

If possible, so far as it depends on you, be at peace with all men.

Romans 12:18

Pursue peace with all men, and the sanctification without which no one will see the Lord.

Hebrews 12:14

At this point you may have some concerns regarding the privacy of sensitive information. If you find yourself engaged in a conversation as a member of the lay ministry, then what is said between the two parties should always be kept confidential. This is in regards to relaying any information outside of the leadership of the church. However, please keep in mind the importance of relaying pertinent information to the Director of Pastoral Care in your report. This is **especially** true in cases of abuse.

Abuse may come in the form of child abuse, sexual abuse, spousal abuse, or elder abuse. Also when there is the potential threat of suicide. These need to be reported promptly to the director of Pastoral Care. This is not a violation of privacy but rather protocol to protect both yourself and the church.

There is one other abuse that I must touch on. It is the matter of spiritual abuse. Spiritual abuse is the misuse of power, authority, or assumed authority to manipulate and control others. This is never to be tolerated. This and any other form of abuse that you become aware of needs to be reported to the Director of the PCM and also documented. The responsibility for this matter then falls to the Director and you are covered by your documentation. Always document and report such matters immediately.

Some of the most basic fundamental needs of the church can be supplied by the Pastoral Care Ministry Team freeing the hands of the senior staff to attend to administrative duties, study, and prayer. A healthy growing church cannot expect the senior pastors to shoulder the burden of the church alone. They need the help of their trained lay leadership.

Discussion

- What is the protocol for reporting abuse or other serious matters?

- How important is confidentiality when ministering to others?

- How would you handle someone who comes to you with a complaint about another church leader?

- If we share information obtained during ministry time, who would we share it with and for what purpose?

How Does The PCM Assist Church Leadership?

I remember many years ago when I lived in Ohio, our church did not have a PCM. All visitations were the responsibility of the senior pastors. This became a huge responsibility, even though the church had less than 150 members. Many of those members were in the seventy and older age bracket with increased needs for pastoral care.

A wonderful team of lay leaders agreed to help and I was honored to become the first Pastoral Care Director in the history of that church. Since I was new to this type of ministry, I was blessed with an opportunity to discuss PCM with several other Pastoral Care Directors. They both had sizable PCM teams in large successful churches. The knowledge I gained from their mentorship, as well as the guidance of my senior pastors was monumental in launching our first PCM.

While some of the information I had gathered did not apply to our smaller congregation, much of it did. It gave me a vision for our PCM both in the immediate future and in the years to come. Vision is important. Our first PCM team was formed, but where to begin? We had a large percentage of widows, widowers, and shut-ins that needed assistance.

Following up on the elderly, shut-ins, nursing home residents or the sick in the hospital is a great place to begin a PCM experience. We created a schedule for visitations each month and each PCM team of two was responsible for one or two visitations per week. Training was mandatory for team members and we planned meetings for the whole team once each month.

Communion was one of the many topics we discussed. Many of the team members had expressed apprehension regarding the giving of communion. They had never served communion before and it made them uncomfortable.

We created a small communion set for the teams to take with them during visitations and included an outline of scriptures and a sample prayer that team members could utilize if they wished. Each kit was in a small carrying case along with the communion elements. We also provided small serving size bottles of grape juice.

Preparation is half of the battle. Once the team members had used the kits several times their anxiety dissipated. Even the newest team members felt at ease when offering communion. The experience helped PCM team members grow in their ministry skills, and the shut-ins that received communion were blessed in the process.

Visitation of shut-ins is only one way PCM can assist the senior pastor. Another important task is keeping track of new visitors and absentees and providing follow-up. The follow up may include giving them a call, sending a note or potentially an email. It is important that new visitors feel welcome and wanted. Equally important is the member who has been absent from the weekly services. They need to know that they were missed and someone cares enough to check in on them.

When inquiring about someone either in the church, on the phone, or during a visitation, we must express our sincere concern without seeming to pry. Keep it simple. Don't press for a lot of details; just gather enough information to pray effectively. Once again, keep it simple. Some use the guise of prayer to accomplish their own agendas even using it to manipulate and control. We never want to be guilty of that whether intentionally or unintentionally. Therefore stick to praying for the needs they have expressed in sincerity.

Visitations

Remember to make visitations as a team. It is not appropriate for a solitary man or woman to do a home visitation especially if the one you are visiting is of the opposite sex. It is best to always use the buddy system when doing home visitations. Nursing homes and hospitals are not so concerning as others are also present however most of the time, team visitation is preferred.

Hospital visitation is a bit different and may require more flexibility and patience by the PCM team. Families of patients who are ill or injured may need consoling and support along with the patient. It is important to respect the families' wishes to the best of your ability. Patients who are facing surgery, in a coma, or on a ventilator may need additional support.

The family may need you to sit with them while their loved one is in surgery, especially if it is a critical case. Be prepared with some scriptures and ready to pray both for the patient and the family as is appropriate.

Families in crisis may unleash their anxiety on anyone that they can, please do not take it personally. Be sensitive to their needs, and understanding of the trauma they are presently experiencing. Do what you can to support them and back away if they do not want you to assist. Do not involve yourself in family matters. Your goal is to promote peace and harmony while strengthening the family unit as a representative of the church.

Nursing homes visits are frequently less challenging than visits to the hospital. The patient in a nursing home is usually there because of long term health problems. For some, it will be the last change of address before going home to be with the Lord. Here perhaps more than ever, you want to make certain the person has had the opportunity to accept the Lord and is at peace that their future home will be with their Heavenly Father.

As in any facility, whether hospital, urgent care, or nursing home one needs to be respectful of facility rules and regulations. As noted before, the staff should not have to stop what they are doing so that you can take time to minister. You want to be an asset to the health care team, not a hindrance.

PCM team members must be fully trained and have a sense of the Senior Pastor's heart. A network of such lay ministers can be a valuable asset to the Pastors and their ministry. They can also be a valuable asset to the body of the church. Utilization of the talents and gifts that God has placed within the body will strengthen and undergird the ministry of the Pastors and keep their flock not only happy, but healthy.

How do we prevent people from falling through the cracks?

1. Follow up on visitors and absentees.

2. Inquire sincerely as to the well-being of those you contact.

3. Listen attentively and minister to their needs:

4. Be diligent not to procrastinate with follow-up.

Pastoral Care Ministry within the Church Walls

PCM can also assist within the four walls of the church. Greeting visitors or by fellowshipping with people who tend to hang on the fringe of the congregation. Working to make everyone feel welcome, wanted, and accepted. It is easy to be caught up in hanging out in groups with those who are familiar. Cliques alienate outsiders. What if we each make a point of drawing others into conversations, inviting them to bible studies and other church wide events?

People who feel welcome and wanted are more likely to return for a second visit. Is your church a friendly church? Or do people feel they do not fit in? Do they feel like no one cares? It is everyone's responsibility to reach out and include others. How do we do that? By creating a loving and caring environment that welcomes the rich and the poor, the politician and the farmer. We are all on equal ground when it comes to joining the family of God.

Let us review:

1. Make a point to welcome visitors, but also greet others from the congregation.

2. Seek them out and introduce yourself.

3. Shake their hands and make certain they get a visitor's packet to fill out.

4. Be attentive to any needs they may express, but do not pry for information.

5. Pray with those who desire it.

6. If any have needs that require counseling or special assistance, please refer them to the Director of the Pastoral Care Team.

7. Make them feel welcome and wanted. Invite them to visit again. Ask if they have a home church or are looking for one.

Ministry within the Community

1. Go two at a time when possible. Men can visit men, or women visit women, or couples can go together to minister to an individual's needs. We want to flee every appearance of evil.

2. Shut-ins may desire communion. Become comfortable in giving communion.

3. Remember who you represent when you go to minister to others.

4. Make certain that the lasting impression you leave with others is a good one.

5. Be respectful of staff and family. Don't expect special treatment.

Discussion

- In your own words, what is body ministry?

- Is pastoral ministry an administrative position?

- Who do the pastoral ministers serve and in what way?

- How might you grow in your gifts and talents via participation in the PCM?

Now you are Christ's body, and individually members of it.

1 Corinthians 12:27

Church Growth Is
Facilitated By Effective PCM

Years ago my family obtained a huge aquarium for our family room. Unfortunately, the floor did not have a sufficient number of joists to adequately support the structure. To compensate for the additional weight, several jacks were placed in strategic locations under the floor. Once in place, the floor was able to withstand the additional weight of the aquarium without sagging. As the responsibilities of senior staff increases, a trained team of pastoral ministers becomes imperative.

The early church grew rapidly after the day of Pentecost. Note how Luke describes the growth process in Acts.

> *Praising God and having favor with all the people. And the Lord was <u>adding</u> to their number day by day those who were being saved.*

> **Acts 2:47**

Later Luke records church growth in terms of multiplication rather than addition.

> *And in those days, when the number of the disciples was <u>multiplied</u>, there arose a murmuring of the Grecians against the Hebrews, because their widows were neglected in the daily ministration.*

> **Acts 6:1 KJV**

> *And the word of God increased; and the number of the disciples <u>multiplied</u> in Jerusalem greatly; and a great company of the priests were obedient to the faith.*

> **Acts 6:7 KJV**

Look at the table on the next page. It documents growth by addition. If four leaders were to disciple 2 new converts every 3 months, within a year one would see 32 new disciples. That is awesome, but it is growth by addition not growth by multiplication.

Church Growth by Addition

1st 3 months 4 people disciple 2 new converts = <u>8 new disciples</u>

2nd 3 months same 4 people disciple 2 more new converts = 8 more new disciples

3rd 3 months same 4 people disciple 2 more new converts= 8 more new converts

4th 3 months same 4people disciple 2 more new converts = 8 more new converts.

4 Leaders discipled a total of **32** new converts in one year.

Now let us consider growth by multiplication. If those same four leaders trained their new converts how to share their faith and disciple others, it might look like this table.

Church Growth by Multiplication

1st 3 months 4 people disciple 2 new converts = <u>8 new disciples</u>

2nd 3 months same 4 people disciple + 8 more new converts for a total of 12 people disciple 2 new converts = 24 more new disciples

3rd 3 months the 12 +24 = 36 people disciple 2 new converts= 72 new converts.

4th 3 months 36 + 72 new believers = 108 disciplers each one mentors 2 new converts = 216 more new converts.

Start out with 4 disciplers, and end of the year you have 324 disciplers.

Growth from 4 to **324** in one year.

How does PCM help in church growth?

Lay leaders are to lead by example. You may or may not be called upon to teach classes, but you mentor best by being a visible example of how a Christian should live their life. If you are a lay leader, you are being watched. Remember from the youngest to the oldest people are taking note of how you handle life.

Are you easily angered? Or are you patient and kind? Do you put on your church clothes and your church attitude on Sunday but the rest of the week you act differently? You may not think anyone will notice, but they will.

We need to make certain that our weekly persona and our Sunday persona are one in the same. We are to serve as a living example of a Christ-like believer. The person who cares for those in the congregation, and in the community needs to be mature in their own walk with the Lord.

PCM also helps to create an environment that is conducive to nurturing others. Creating a nurturing environment begins with a willingness to listen to concerns, pray for needs, offer words of encouragement, lay hands on the sick, and strengthening in the word. When people feel wanted and accepted they will begin to communicate their needs and concerns. Communication is key.

People also need to sense a high level of integrity from the PCM team as this cultivates trust. Trust opens the door to communication. Once two-way communication is activated, they can easily be guided from new believer to mature disciple and eventually leader. This is more than growth by numbers, it is growth by maturation. Mature believers are capable of fulfilling their place in the body and exercising their gifts.

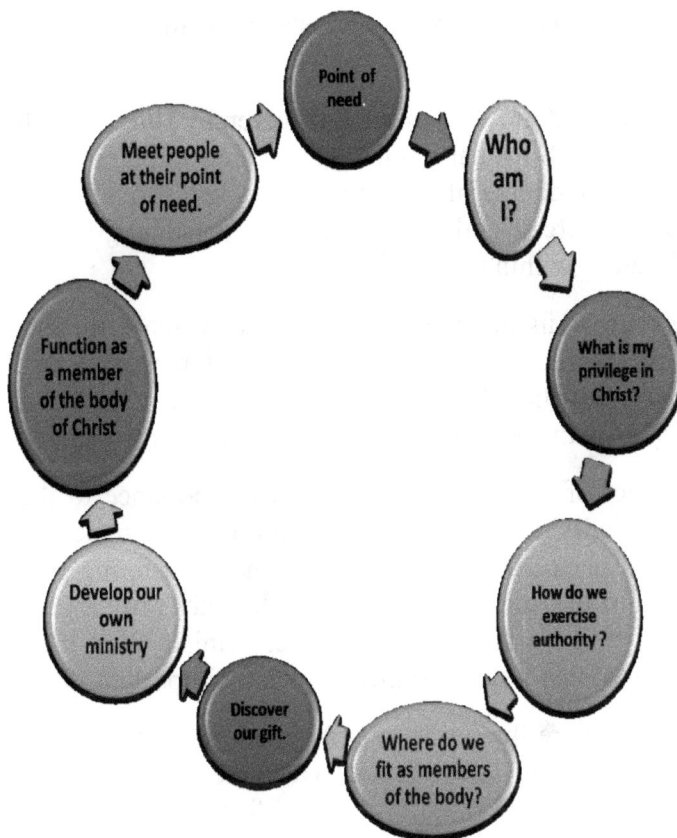

Personal Growth through Ministry Opportunities

The diagram above illustrates the cycle of growth for an individual believer. The point of need at the top is the beginning of the cycle. An individual needs to recognize their need for a savior. Once they have accepted the Lord, they need to discover who they are in Christ. As the cycle continues, the individual believer discovers their personal inheritance and the authority they have as a child of God.

As the believer matures, they need to find their place in the body and become equipped to do the work which God has called them to do. This is aided through the assistance of members of the five-fold ministry.

Discovering and growing in the gifts given by Holy Spirit helps the believer grow. Spiritual maturity can come through opportunities realized in the course of daily ministry. Members within the PCM are able to exercise and utilize their own personal gifts to minister to individuals within the body.

As they grow in these gifts, their own personal ministries will begin to emerge. Discovery of and development of one's own personal motivational gift and spiritual gifts is important for both personal growth, and the growth of the body as a whole.

The subject of gifts is a topic of grave importance to the church and to the individual members of the church. The understanding of one's own personal motivational gift and ministering through the operation of that gift will help the whole body work together more effectively; like a well-oiled machine. Ministry that includes the exercising of one's spiritual gifts is equally important.

Briefly, there are three sets of gifts given to us by the Father, the Son, and by the Holy Spirit. God the father gives us our motivational gift, also known as a lifestyle or personality gift. Jesus gave the gift of the five-fold ministry to the church for the equipping of the saints. Holy Spirit gives each of us several spiritual gifts to empower us for ministry. For more on discovering your gifts, refer to the book, *Treasures of the Heart*.[12]

Why should I become a member of the PCM?

1. A healthy church should also be growing <u>scripturally</u>, spiritually, <u>educationally</u>, emotionally, and socially.

---

[12] *Treasures of the Heart Gifts of the Trinity* by Kathy J. Smith published by Vision Publishing, 1115 D Street Ramona CA 92065

2. A church's <u>numerical growth</u> can be stunted if the members of its body do not take responsibility for their own <u>spiritual growth</u> and development.

3. Spiritual growth can come through opportunities realized in the course of daily ministry.

4. Opportunities to lead by example come through PCM.

5. As the church body grows <u>numerically</u> more and more of the everyday care for the members will need to become the responsibility of the individuals in the PCM.

PCM can be the <u>proving ground</u> for other ministry opportunities.

Discussion

- How can you use your gifts to benefit the body of Christ?

- What are some of the ways the church can grow through effective PCM?

- What is the difference between growth by addition and growth by multiplication, and how might one use this information to help the church grow both numerically and spiritually?

Goals of Pastoral Ministry

The goal of pastoral care is to restore health, healing, and comfort. It is to strengthen and equip the believer and their family to be all that they were called to be. This can only be accomplished in an environment where he or she feels safe, secure, and respected. We are to be a healing community where the lost, hurt, and broken come to be healed.

PCM is to be an extension of the pastor's caring ministry reaching out into the community when appropriate through visitation of the sick, widowed, and house bound individuals. They are to uphold the patients and their families in hospitals, nursing homes, and other residential facilities including jail and prison. They stand alongside of the grieving and may assist in funerals when asked by the PCM director.

The long range goal of PCM is to be a representative of the church under the pastor's authority bringing the love of Jesus to those in need. Those chosen to participate in such ministry opportunities need to be qualified to serve.

> *The Lord therefore said to Moses, "Gather for Me seventy men from the elders of Israel, whom you know to be the elders of the people and their officers and bring them to the tent of meeting, and let them take their stand there with you. Then I will come down and speak with you there, and I will take of the Spirit who is upon you, and will put Him upon them; and they shall bear the burden of the people with you, so that you will not bear it all alone.*

Numbers 11:16-17

Some of the biblical qualifications found in James 1:27 and Isaiah 58:6-10 for lay leaders include:

Blameless	Not argumentative.
Sober minded	Possess proper motivation.
Good mannered or well behaved.	Patient and full of grace.
Must love all people!	Not a novice.
Must be able to teach.	Must be in good standing and of good report both in and outside of the church
Not a drunkard	

Discussion

- Why are the qualities of leaders listed above important?

- What goals do you have for participating in the PCM?

- What challenges do you anticipate as you move forward to take a part in your local PCM?

What responsibilities
will I be asked to perform?

Responsibilities differ from church to church as determined by the church leadership. Some tasks that could be included are: visiting shut-ins, widows, hospital visitation, and jail and/or prison ministry. Follow up on absentees, welcoming new guests, all the while maintaining a loving, caring, environment within the church. You may need to represent the PCM at the funeral home, or even participate in the funeral service when asked by your PCM Director.

Once again, responsibilities are assigned by the director of Pastoral Care in accordance with the pastor's wishes. You may be asked to help in any or all of the above tasks. In addition, certain reports need to be filled out such as visitation reports. Please do so in a timely manner.

There are certain concerns that need to be reported immediately; such as cases of possible abuse or suicide. In such cases, please notify your director quickly while maintaining the privacy of the individual involved in the report.

Calling and leaving a message on a voice mail or with a receptionist is not appropriate. Please ask the director of your PCM directly how he or she would like you to communicate such emergencies to them, and follow their instructions.

Housekeeping Items

Clergy may have special privileges in public institutions including parking in specific areas, or access to free parking. There may or may not be a prayer room or chapel accessible to members of the clergy. If you must park in a parking garage with hourly fees, stop at the front desk and introduce yourself to the staff. Be certain you have an identification that proves your affiliation with the PCM and your title. If fees for parking are waived for Lay Ministers they should be able to assist you. Please check with your leadership for more specific details in your area.

Remember that you represent the church, the pastors, and ultimately the Lord to the community. Do not request special treatment. Respect the staff and their need to complete their work. Remember to be cordial. Check with the staff before visiting a patient in a hospital or nursing home. Remember to avoid going when you have been sick yourself. Good hand washing practices are a must to prevent the spread of disease to yourself and others.

Note: There may be specific requirements for entrance to patient's rooms that are in critical care, cardiac care or other specialized units. Patients with contagious conditions may also require special precautions. Be sensitive to the rules and regulations of the facility in which you are serving.

Jails and or prisons have a specific process you must adhere to in order to gain entrance to their facility. Familiarize yourself with the requirements of the unit you will be visiting to insure you remain in compliance as a faithful representative of the Lord.

Job Description

The Pastoral Care Ministry is to care for the church as designated by the Senior Pastors. PCM team members' primary responsibility is to the Director of the Pastoral Care Ministry and he/she is responsible to the Senior Pastors.

The PCM Director takes responsibility for scheduling visitations and reviewing the reports of all visits. He or she then reports this information directly to the Pastors. This allows the head of the church to continue to monitor what is happening within the body via the communication of the PCM team.

It is by virtue of the activities and communication of the PCM that a sense of unity and cohesiveness can be maintained within the body no matter how big the body becomes. You too can have a happy, healthy, growing church. No more people falling through the cracks or missing in action when an effective Pastoral Care Ministry team is at work. Senior Pastors no longer need to feel overwhelmed and overworked by the demands of their flock.

Visitation and follow-up of their constituents can be managed by the PCM. This will free up their schedule and allow them more time for prayer and study of the word. Who knows, perhaps they will even have more time to spend with their spouse and families. That would be a wonderful thing indeed.

We are the ambassadors for Christ...

"Therefore we are ambassadors for Christ, as though God were entreating through us; we beg you on behalf of Christ, be reconciled to God,"

II Corinthians 5:20 NASB

Conclusion

But Moses' hands were heavy. Then they took a stone and put it under him, and he sat on it; and Aaron and Hur supported his hands, one on one side and one on the other. Thus his hands were steady until the sun set.

Exodus 17:2

As Aaron and Hur held up Moses' hands in the battle against the Amelekites, Israel prevailed. It is the job of the PCM to hold up the hands of the church leadership. Your job is not to serve "the institutional church" and your job is not to serve the people.

Saul served the people and lost a kingdom. Absalom started serving the people and started a rebellion. You will be involved in ministry to the people; but your primary responsibility is to the Pastors.

As you minister to the people through the authority of the pastors, you are in fact, holding up their arms. You are lightening their load and growing in your own gifts and calling as well. It is a winning combination for the church, for the church leaders, and for you.

Remember the diagram of the tree with all the roots? It takes a healthy root system to grow a tree. It takes a healthy PCM to enable the church to grow. Growth is not about numbers, but more importantly it is about growing in maturity. It is a mature church that begins to bear fruit.

One of the very first commandments God gave to man was this, be fruitful and multiply (Genesis 1:28). Now is the time for each of us to be about our Father's work.

A fruitful church is one with a strong and healthy root system. As you do the work of the ministry under the guidance of the pastors, you create an intricate and growing network of roots. This healthy foundation rooted in the Lord will enable the church to grow and bear the fruit of the kingdom.

Remember, above all we are here to serve the Lord. We are to be his hands and his feet. We are to share the love and the joy of the Lord with all that we meet, to help those who are less fortunate. Pray for the sick, feed the poor, do the work of the ministry and occupy until Jesus returns.

Sincerely,

Kathy J. Smith

Resources

Books

Leadership In The Church by Dr, Stan DeKoven

The Healing Community by Dr. Stan DeKoven

Treasures of the Heart by Kathy Smith

Walk In Wisdom by Dr. Stan DeKoven

Wisdom Speaks by Kathy Smith

<u>Student Study Guide</u> for Effective Pastoral Care in the Local Church

Certificate Programs by Vision International

www.vision.edu

Chaplaincy

Pastoral Ministry

Websites

www.careministry.com

www.booksbyvision.com

www.planpurposedestiny.org

www.ingramcontent.com/pod-product-compliance
Lightning Source LLC
Chambersburg PA
CBHW060145050426
42448CB00010B/2300